Possum Ranch Parables

A ficticious story of an imaginary world,
parables, if you will, which teach the basic
principles of life in my own way,
rather than the traditional way
people use to convey relationsip
between God and mankind

Pamela Dickson

I

Dedication

I want to dedicate this book to my husband Michael, because it was his idea.

Were it not for his constant encouragement, steadfast help, and confidence in me, I would not be doing any of the things I do today.

Michael also is the first person ever to show me what unconditional love looks like, I had never seen it, so I'd never been able to give it to others or receive it from God on a consistent basis.

The only person more responsible for totally changing my life for the better than Michael is Jesus.

We will celebrate our 22nd wedding anniversary this year, proof that God never gives up on anybody who'll give Him a chance.

I may answer to Missfit, but Michael treats me like a princess!

I'll always love you Michael,

Pam

ISBN: 1-4392-0281-8
ISBN-13: 9781439202814

Visit www.booksurge.com
http://www.booksurge.com> to order additional copies.

Preface

Merkie and Missfit are Mike and Pam Dickson and their Possum Ranch is located in Claypool, Indiana.

Possum Ranch Puppets and Clowns began as a ministry only, but now has branched out to include campgrounds, company picnics, fairs, parties, concerts, car shows etc.

They travel to these events in their own brightly decorated yellow box truck and they also have a cool clown car they drive in area parades.

Kids (of all ages!) love their puppet shows, skits, magic tricks, music, games, ventriloquism, audience participation and especially their latest endeavor... totally awesome "full face" painting.

Pam also writes and sings parodies, expressing how she and Mike's lives were, before and after trusting God.

Contact information:

Voice Mail: (574) 372-0574
Email: possumranch@kconline.com
Web site: www.possumranch.com

Table of Contents

Introduction

Because I was misled, I saw myself as a misfit.

I didn't discover this misconception until my misconduct had already caused me to make many mistakes.
Being misguided by misgivings led to mishap after mishap.

My misunderstanding of the true nature of God opened the door for mischief to reign.
My misdeeds were a direct result of a misconstrued belief system.

An absent mischievous father and a precious but misguided mother, (who's names were Mr. and Mrs. Wright) unknowingly misdirected me to literally misdoubt God's goodness.

Consequently, misfortune & misery were constant companions in the misadventure called my life.
This misapprehension caused me to misbelieve and miscalculate the trustworthiness of not only every human

being on the face of the earth, but especially God Himself.

Misnamed Pamela, (which means "All Honey") was a misnomer misspent on me, Mr. and Mrs. Wright's misfit.

Growing up in a destructive belief system which practiced misuse of God's mysterious ways by misrule, caused my misplaced allegiance to be on misguided people who actually mistreat misinformed misfits.

My misbehaving nearly caused me to miss it, but one day I finally discovered that God so loves misfits, that He sent a mystery from heaven, (named Jesus), with a mission not only to seek and to save the lost, but also to restore every single thing that had been missing in their lives.

Be very careful not to misinterpret His motives!
I'd hate to see you miss out on your blood bought inheritance, because when it's all said and done, this life is just a mist!

With love, Missfit

Chapter 1

Firm Foundation

"Possum Ranch" is the name Merkie the clown affectionately began calling the rugged five acre plot he and Missfit had bought in order to build a home someday.

What's funny is that back then they had no idea that Mr. Perkins Possum and Miss Pearly Mae Possum actually already lived in their woods!

It wasn't long before they all became acquainted with each other though.
Merkie still teases Missfit about the first time she caught sight of Pearly Mae!

You see, before moving into their new home on the Possum Ranch, Missfit had always lived in the city, so the first time she got a glimpse of a live possum, thinking it to be a very big RAT, she screamed at the top of her lungs and went
running off so fast you'd have thought a hungry bear was after her!
That was several years ago, but Missfit still accuses Merkie of laughing way too hard over the whole incident!

Not long after that, Merkie discarded a couple of great big old dog houses out in their woods, and unknown to either clown, the possums each chose one to use for their own homes.

Today spring is in the air and there's no happier time out on the Possum Ranch, especially after having to endure an unusually harsh winter like this one had been!
Perkins the possum even decided to stay up after day break, and go for a run. Because Possums are nocturnal they usually spend all day sleeping you know...but not this day!

Merkie was outside on his tractor, also enjoying the welcome warm spring air.
He was using a long pole with a hook on the end of it to pick up an entire winter's worth of trash that uncaring people had thrown out of their car windows along the road, when he spotted Perkins jogging along the tree line. He couldn't believe his eyes!
He immediately put his tractor in reverse and spun around to greet him, but Possums are really quick on their feet you know!

"I know what I'll do!" Merkie thought to himself, "I'll blow my whistle!"
Merkie always wears his whistle around his neck because, as he says, "You just never know when you're going to need to whistle for a friend."

Perkins stopped fast in his tracks as soon as he heard Merkie's whistle, and each one headed towards the other.
4

"Howdy!" Perkins hollered over the engine noise, "How yawl doing on this here fine day?"

Merkie joked as he reached to turn the throttle down. "I'm good Mr. Perkins, just glad to still be on the green side of the sod!"

"Me too!" said Perkins, "I just got over having the flu though, which is why I'm out jogging."

"What?" Merkie shouted, while turning off the engine.
"Yup," started Perkins, "I heard somewhere that aerobic exercise kills disease-causing bacteria, but I never could figure out how to make them there bacteria agree to exercise!"

Merkie and Missfit and all of their Possum Ranch family had come to expect some sort of funny punch line from Perkins nearly every time he showed up and this had endeared him to them.

"That's funny!" Merkie laughed while at the same time detecting an unpleasant odor. Holding onto his big red nose he complained,
"Pew, what's that horrible smell?"

Perkins sniffed at the air, and then at himself saying, "Hum...I'm afraid it's me, sorry!
I reckon I need a bath after all that there jogging!
See yawl later."

He scurried towards what he now was very proud and happy to call his very own little possum house, in

Merkie & Missfit's woods.

Perkins had just headed for the bath tub that Merkie had rigged up for him, when he heard something outside.

Running to the door he saw a truck rumbling up the drive
"Goody! That's probably the repair man I called yesterday," He thought to himself.

Hearing "Knock-knock-knock," he said, "Come on in," Continuing with, "pardon the stink, but I just finished jogging and I'm a bit sweaty."

"Oh, that's alright," answered the Repair Man, "just point me towards what needs repaired."

"Shore enough! It's my walls, and my ceiling, see them there cracks?" Perkins pointed out, "They're everywhere."

Mr. Repair Man had a look around before asking, "Mind if I check outside?"

"Go right ahead sir!" Perkins agreed, "I'm going to jump into the tub while you do, if it's ok."

"No problem," He replied.

Perkins took a nice cold bath and dried off just in time to hear Mr. Repair Man back at the front door. "I'm sorry Mr. Perkins, but I can't be of any help to you," said the man.

6

"I don't need yawl to help me! I just need you to fix those confounded cracks," Perkins said with a wink.

"Those cracks aren't really your problem sir," answered the repair man.

"Just who's problem do you suppose they are then?" Perkins blinked.

"Oh, they're your problem alright Mr. Perkins, but it's all because your foundation is sinking because, well sir, a foundation needs to be strong and solid," The repair man dropped his gaze down to the floor and apologetically said, "Frankly sir, yours is nothing but sand."

Perkins questioned, "Sand?"

"Yes sir" he replied looking back up, "Sinking sand!"

Perkins drew back in disbelief, "OH NO! This is serious trouble!"

"I'm really sorry Mr. Perkins," said the Repair man.

"So am I! Thanks anyway for your trouble," Answered the unhappy possum as he showed him out.
Turning around and heading for the kitchen, Perkins sighed, "Woe is me! A sinking foundation! I wonder if it could cause my whole house to collapse."
Putting a pot of water on the fire to make some dry leaf tea, he had just sat down in his favorite chair when he heard, "ROAR!"

Running to the door, he saw that it was Leo, his Lion friend.

"Shush!" Perkins demanded, "Don't make any sudden movements! My house is sinking!"

"Oh that's easy to fix!" beamed Leo, "I always boil potpourri… that stuff really clears the air!"

"It's not stinking! It's sinking!" Perkins cried as he gave his tail a shake.
"Whoops, sorry," Leo snickered, "Merkie said you were down here washing off the stink, so I just assumed…."

Perkins despaired, "My house is sinking because my foundation is nothing but sand!"

"Whoa!" responded Leo, "That's REALLY not cool!"

"Forgive me Leo; I'm not being a very good host. Won't you come in and share a cup of tea with me?" Perkins asked as he backed out of the doorway, "Just promise you won't roar."

"Thanks Perkins," Leo responded looking around, "It won't cave in on us will it?"
Then he smiled big as he had a thought. "Hey, didn't Jesus say something about that when He was here?"
Doing a double take, Perkins marveled, "Jesus…was here!?"

"Not HERE!" Leo went on, "I mean when He was here on the earth 2000 years ago."

"How would I know?" Perkins mused, "I hadn't been born yet!"

Feeling compassion for his friend Leo began, "I'll tell you what I DO know Perkins!"

"What's that?" He asked.

"My mom says her faith in God was a rock solid foundation for her when she became a widow."

Perkins wasn't listening too well as he was busy grinding the tea leaves and responded, "I like your mom! She's not a weirdo!"

Laughing out loud, Leo almost roared, "She's NOT a weirdo, she's a widow!"

"Whoops, sorry!" Perkins apologized with a toothy grin, adding, "Shush!"

Leo whispered, "My Mom says that God promises in His Word to be a defender of widows and a Father to the Fatherless! And she says I'm living proof that He keeps His promises too."

Perkins was quick to reply, "Well that's nice Leo, but I sure enough don't see what in tar nation that has to do with my cracking walls!"

"Faith Perkins, it's all about faith in God." Leo insisted as he lapped up the last of his tea, "I'd better get going, but thanks so much for the tea, good bye."

As he left the woods and headed across the yard, Leo spotted Merkie, still out on his tractor. Stopping he called out, "ROAR! Merkie ole buddy ole pal... ROAR!"

Merkie easily heard Leo's roar above his tractor noise and drove down the driveway to say hello.
"What's up friend?" Merkie asked.

"Mr. Perkins is not himself today!" Leo complained.

"Not himself?" Merkie contemplated, "I just spoke with him, and other than stinking a bit, he was fine."

Leo exaggerated, "He's acting just like my cousin who swallowed a frog!"
"Whoa! I'm thinking that'd make you good and sick," Merkie cringed.

"Sick," Leo sat down, "He's liable to croak any minute!"

Merkie saw the twinkle in Leo's eyes and realized he was having some fun with him.
"Ha," He snorted, throwing his head back together with Leo as they shared a good belly laugh together.
"Seriously," Merkie noted," I noticed some guy visiting Perkins earlier."

Straightening up Leo said, "Perkins said the repairman says his walls are cracking because the foundation beneath his house is sinking, and now Perkins whole attitude is sinking."

"Not to worry!" Merkie's eyes brightened, "If Mr. Perkins is feeling down, I know just what he needs! Pearly Mae always cheers him up."

"Say no more!" cheered Leo, "I'll find her!" And so he set about to find Miss Pearly Mae possum.

He thought she might be asleep since it was daylight, but he risked knocking at her door just the same. As it happens, she was still up, washing the breakfast dishes.
As soon as Leo told her that Perkins needed some cheering up, she dropped what she was doing and went to pay him a visit.

Chapter 2

What Perkins Doesn't Know!

Pearly Mae stuck her snout inside Perkins house and hollered, "Anybody home?"

"Just one poor pitiful possum," came back.

Pearly Mae asked as she waddled in, "What seems to be ailing you, Possum pal of mine?"

"Just when I thought things couldn't possibly get any worse, sure enough, they went and got worse!" Perkins sighed.

"Well, you could eat a live toad first thing in the morning, and then nothing worse can happen to you the rest of the day!" Pearly Mae teased.

Perkins frowned, "Oh believe me, it's something worse alright!"

Pearly Mae insisted, "Are you sure? Or are you over reacting some?"
"I don't think so. I'd say having my house collapse because it was built on sinking sand is bad enough," Perkins explained.

Unscathed, Pearly Mae continued, "Now Mr. Perkins, calm down. There is one place you can always go for some powerful good news, if you'd allow me the privilege of telling you what's in your bible."

"Oh, I already know everything that's in MY Bible," Perkins boasted uncaringly.

"You do?" Pearly Mae gasped in disbelief, "Good grief, I guess you'd best tell me then!"

Perkins started, "OK! There's a picture of my brothers girl-friend, a ticket from the dry cleaners, one of my curls, and a Pizza Hut coupon!"

Pearly Mae couldn't hold back a giggle, "Land Sakes Perkins! Not what's in YOUR bible, I mean in THE bible. Besides, is that all you know about your bible?"
"Of course not," Perkins defended, "I know that the first pair ate the first apple!"

Pearly Mae bristled, "Don't you know that it says God is close to the brokenhearted?"

Perkins sighed, "I guess."

"You guess? Don't you know Jesus told His disciples that He would be with them always, even to the end of the age?" she went on.

"But I can't see him!" Perkins said while looking up, "I shore do see my cracking walls and ceiling though!"

Pearly Mae continued, "Perkins, the bible says in 2 Corinthians 4:18 "to fix our eyes not on what is seen, but on what is unseen. For what is seen is temporary (and changeable) but what is unseen is eternal."

Still looking up towards his ceiling Perkins said, "Just how does a fellow fix his eyes on something he can't see?"

"Through faith Perkins," Pearly Mae almost whispered, "faith in a good God. You see, what ever you focus your thoughts on will grow bigger and bigger in your mind. You can focus on your problems, or you can focus on your problem solver, it's your choice. Personally, I've learned if you pray and present your requests in Jesus' name, your prayers will be answered."

Perkins looked down saying, "Oh, I've heard Jesus promises to give new lives for old and warm hearts for cold, but how's that going to help me with my sinking house?"

Pearly Mae backed up and twitching her whiskers said, "I'm not sure, but just ask Him and trust Him with it, and you'll find out!
Now if you'll excuse me, it's time for me to go and play possum....bye now."

Looking up Perkins forced a smile saying, "Thanks for trying to encourage me, good friend of mine."

Pearly Mae let herself out, while silently praying, asking God to help Perkins with this dilemma.

She returned home and was just about to doze off to sleep when she heard hound dog barking like crazy! "For heaven's sake," she exclaimed, "He should know it's my bedtime!"

She waddled to the doorway to see what was causing such a ruckus, just in time to catch Perkins disappearing behind his house. He was waving his front paws frantically in the air. All the while Hound Dog was barking, almost as though something had frightened him.

"This day is becoming very burdensome." Pearly Mae thought to herself. "I'll never get to sleep at this rate! Hmm…This calls for the beast of burden himself, ole Mr. Camel!"

She headed for the main house, hoping Missfit would answer the door, and she did.

"Oh good," replied Pearly Mae. "I was hoping you'd answer! I need to get some shut eye!"

"What are you doing up? She asked, "It's nearly noon!"

"You mean to tell me you can't hear Hound Dogs barking?" Pearly Mae complained.

Missfit turned to look out back, and sure enough, Hound Dog was running around in circles, barking his head off.

"What's he barking at?" She asked.

"I have no idea! This day is becoming very burdensome!" She complained through a yawn.

"Ah! Say no more…this calls for the beast of burden himself, Clyde the Camel! I'll send him out right away!" Missfit promised.

"That's why I love you Missfit! Thank you." And she headed back home to the woods.

Meanwhile, Missfit skipped down to the barn calling, "Are you out here Clyde?"

"I'm here" was his answer, "Worlds best beast of burden, at your service!"

"Thanks Clyde," she said, "You are the best! Pearly Mae just visited me and said this day is becoming burdensome because she can't get to sleep and I immediately thought of you. Would you mind going out to the kennel to see what's causing Hound Dog to bark so?"

"I don't mind at all! You know lifting burdens is my passion," Clyde answered as he brushed past her and headed off towards the woods.
Missfit thanked the Lord for sending Clyde to them, (which is another whole story.)
God rewarded her gratitude with an entire morning to herself. (Psalm 18:36)
Recalling a time when her life was full of chaos and lacking any resemblance of peace, she knew this day was a gift from a God of love, to her.

Chapter 3

"Perkins & the Invisible Elephant"

Clyde the Camel was just about to give Hound Dog a piece of his mind for barking so, when he noticed Perkins racing around his house, waving his paws frantically in the air. Perkins never even saw Clyde coming.
When he got closer he could hear Perkins wailing "Woe is me! Woe is me!"

Finally Clyde called out, "Hey Mr. Perkins, how are you doing?"

"Yikes" Perkins jumped, "You startled me! How am I doing what?"

Clyde continued, "How do you find yourself today?"

"Find myself," Perkins pondered, "I never lost myself!"

Coming to a stop Clyde went on, "You act like you can't understand me."

This time Perkins stopped too, but he still had both front paws in the air, "I'm not acting!"

Clyde, remaining very polite continued, "How do you feel today?"

"I feel... with my paws of course!" Perkins said tilting his head, "Haven't you got anything better to do than bother me with silly questions?"

"Sorry, say, what's that you're so frantically hanging on to there?" Clyde asked.

"Oh that, it's my elephant," Perkins mumbled.

Now Clyde howled out loud, "Right! And I'm Elvis Presley."

"I'm serious!" Perkins stiffened, "Haven't you ever had a stray dog show up out of no where that you couldn't get rid of no matter how hard you tried?"

Clyde grinned big, "Yes, as a matter of fact I did once and it snapped at me so I named it Ginger. Get it? Ginger snaps?"
Unimpressed Perkins groaned, "Whatever..."

"What's the elephant's name?" Clyde asked with an even bigger grin.

"His name is Worry, and he refuses to leave!" Perkins wailed.

"His name is Worry?" Clyde finally understood, "I get it now! Worry is like that, you know! It can make you imagine things that don't even exist."

"Don't exist?" Perkins despaired, "Try telling HIM that!"
He seemed to be fighting with something huge on the end of a leash, but Clyde couldn't see anything!
"Don't do that!" Perkins said to the invisible pest, "See? He's real! He's just invisible."

Clyde couldn't take it any more, "An invisible pet elephant! Don't you mean an imaginary pet elephant? Honestly Perkins, I'd think you'd have enough REAL challenges to face every day, without creating imaginary ones.

Perkins moaned, "Just because you can't see him does not mean he isn't real!" Looking down Perkins continued, "Oh no! I think he just went potty on the side walk!"

By now Clyde was getting exasperated, "No-it-did-not! Listen Perkins, Jesus is bigger than any Worry you have, and He commanded us not to worry! You need to stop this silliness right now. In fact, constant worry is proof that you're letting the devil control you!"

That got Perkins' attention enough that he looked away from the tugging leash and said, "Devil? I don't see any devil!"

"You can't see radio waves either," Clyde suggested, "But I think from the way you're carrying on there that you've been tuned in to his frequency!"

Perkins put one front paw down on the ground while continuing to hold on tight to the leash with the other one, saying, "The devil has a radio station?" "It's bigger than a radio station! It's a world wide frequency of evil that transmits day and night. When you hold on to worry, it actually opens up the door for the devil's thought frequency's to come into your mind to steal, kill, and destroy your life!" (John 10:10)

Perkins was listening intently as he struggled to hang

on to the wildly flailing leash. Then looking at Clyde he asked, "Are you saying he gets into my thoughts and makes me worry?"

Clyde's heart leaped in his chest as he realized Perkins understood, saying, "I just happen to have an instruction book on worry! Would you like to see it?"

"Oh yes!" Perkins agreed, "I've just GOT to get rid of Worry, it's wearing me out!"

Clyde bent all the way down on his knees so Perkins could reach into his saddle bag, saying, "Here you go, it's in there."

Looking inside while still hanging on with both paws to the wild leash, Perkins declared, "That's a bible! I've never read anything about elephants in the Bible!"
Shaking his head Clyde bristled, "If you've ever read anything in the Bible you'd know that it says that worriers must turn every care into a prayer, leave it with God, and stop right there!"

"Hmmm, it does? I'll try anything!" Perkins finally agreed. "Dear God, would you please take this elephant?" he prayed.

As soon as the words left his mouth, it seemed as if the invisible pest must have reared up because Perkins was forced backwards, and almost lost his balance.

"It didn't work!" He said in a high pitched frightened
22

tone.

Clyde was astonished! "Wow, Worry is real! Hey, I think I know what's wrong!
You probably didn't let go of him! You've got to give Worry to God and LEAVE it there!

"Let go of it!?" Perkins declared, "But it could hurt someone!"

Clyde was losing his patience, "Ok, I got it now! You don't really believe God do you!"

"I do so believe in God." Perkins retorted.
"That's not what I said." Clyde scolded, "Lots of people believe IN God, but not many actually believe God.
In Hebrews 11:6 God's Word says "without faith it's impossible to please God, because anyone who comes to Him must believe that He exists and that He rewards those who earnestly seek him."

"He does what?" Perkins cheered.

"God rewards faith Mr. Perkins," Clyde said softly.
"Have you ever heard of Jachobed?"

Distracted, Perkins responded, "Nope, I've heard of a water bed, and an air bed and even a feather bed, but never a jock-oh-bed."

"Too funny," Clyde chuckled, "Jachobed is the name of the mother of Moses and her faith in God helped her to let go of her worry."

"I'd like to hear her story," Perkins softened.
Clyde began, "It's found in Exodus 1 and it goes like this:"

"The king of Egypt had put slave masters over the Israelites to oppress them with forced labor and work them ruthlessly. But the more they were oppressed, the more they multiplied, so the Egyptians came to dread the Israelites.
They made their lives more and more bitter with hard labor in brick and mortar and with all kinds of work in the fields.
One day the king of Egypt said to the Hebrew midwives, "When you help the Hebrew women in childbirth, if it is a boy, kill him; but if it is a girl, let her live."
The midwives, however, feared God and did not do what the king of Egypt had told them to do; they let the boys live.
So God was kind to the midwives and the people increased and became even more numerous. And because the midwives feared God, He gave them families of their own..."

"In other words..." Clyde added, "God rewarded their faith in Him." Going on he continued:
"Jachobed gave birth to a son, and she hid him for three months. But when she could hide him no longer, she got a papyrus basket for him and coated it with tar and pitch. Then she placed the child in it and put it among the reeds along the bank of the Nile. His sister stood at a distance to see what would happen to him."

"You see, Jachobed not only believed IN God, but she believed God!" Clyde added, "And she knew that His plans were to give hope and a future to her people. Anyway..."

"Just then Pharaoh's daughter went down to the Nile to bathe, and her attendants were walking along the river bank. She saw the basket among the reeds and sent her slave girl to get it. She opened it and saw the baby. He was crying, and she felt sorry for him. "This is one of the Hebrew babies," she said. Then his sister asked Pharaoh's daughter," Shall I go and get one of the Hebrew women to nurse the baby for you?"
"Yes, go" she answered. And the girl went and got the baby's mother, Jachobed.
Pharaoh's daughter said to her, "Take this baby and nurse him for me and I will pay you." So the woman took the baby and nursed him.
When the child grew older, she took him to Pharaoh's daughter and he became her son. She named him Moses, saying "I drew him out of the water."

"Wow!" Perkins exclaimed, "God really did honor Jachobeds faith!"

"You can always trust God with your burdensome worry problem Mr. Perkins," Clyde continued, "It says in the bible that Jesus said:

"COME UNTO ME ALL WHO LABOR AND ARE HEAVY

LADENED AND I WILL GIVE YOU REST, FOR MY YOKE IS EASY AND MY BURDEN IS LIGHT!"

And believe me, we camels know all about bearing heavy burdens!"

"Hmmm" Said Perkins, "I guess you should...."
     "Yup!" said Clyde, "Now I'm going to go, but remember, you need to let go of worry, see you later!"

Clyde left Perkins alone to make his decision.
As he walked past Hound Dog's kennel he asked him to please shush, which he did at once because Hound Dog really is a good boy.

Mean while, bowing his head, Perkins prayed, "Dear Jesus, would you please take worry for me?"

Looking up he continued, "Now Worry, I'm going to leave you here with Jesus, and you'll be just fine!"

Perkins let go of the leash and it fell, limp, to the ground!
"WOW!" He said with glee, "I guess WORRY is carrying a burden that God never intended me to bear!"

Picking up the limp leash, feeling a bit worn out, he headed back inside.

Pondering to himself about what a day this had been, he headed off to bed, no longer fearful about his house.

He said a prayer thanking God for taking Worry from him and fell sound asleep as soon as his head hit the pillow!

Proverbs 10:24

"What the wicked dreads will overtake him;
What the righteous desire will be granted."

Chapter 4

A Talking Donkey

Missfit was in the back yard hanging up wet laundry when she saw Owl swooping down out of the tallest tree in the woods.

Seeing their giant bow ties, bold striped socks and bright silk shirts waving in the breeze on the clothes line, Owl shouted, "I see you're taking advantage of God's invisible clothes dryer today."

"Yes," exclaimed Missfit, "The wind is perfect for drying laundry today… and it's free."

Owl hopped up on the fence post and then fluttered down into the fenced in back yard saying, "I'm going to go for a quick fly around the neighborhood after lunch myself!"

"Does the breeze help you to fly?" Missfit inquired. "Oh yes, a slight breeze is very helpful," answered Owl. Then he got a very serious and wise look on his face as he continued, "Do you know that the wind carries sound upwards?"

"What did you hear?" Missfit asked Owl.

"As I listened today it occurred to me that even though the wind is invisible, no one ever doubts that it's real. And yet many of us doubt that God and angels and the devil are real, just because they can't be seen."

"That's pretty deep thinking little friend of mine," Missfit smiled and went on, "That makes me think of Balaam!"

"Who's Balaam?" Owl asked.

Missfit began, "I'm surprised a Wise Owl like you doesn't know about him! Balaam is a man in the Bible who came from the same area in Mesopotamia that Abraham and Sarah came from. But he'd practiced pagan sorcery most of his life. Back then they used to look at the livers and organs of dead animals to predict the future."

"Yummy!" Owl drooled.

"I'd say yucky!" Missfit cringed, adding, "Anyway, Balaam became a believer in the true God and His Angels the day God made his donkey talk!" She chuckled.

"HOOOOO-HOOOO," Howled Owl, "I'd like to hear a story like that!"

Missfit opened her phone to check the time asking, "Do you have a minute?"

"I've always got time for you Missfit."

30

Putting the last piece of clothing on the line, she added, "Would you like to have a seat there on the patio while I go get my bible?"

Owl scurried on over to the picnic table to wait and Missfit came back out carrying her bible and a great big graham cracker for him.

"OK, after Moses led the Israelites out of Egypt, they camped in the dessert. Balaam's story is found in the 22nd chapter of Numbers and goes like this," she began, as she sat down with Owl at the table.
        "The Israelites were camped along the Jordan River across from Jericho and had asked the King of Moab for permission to pass through their land. Moab was fearful and said "NO!"
In fact it says, all of Moab was terrified because there were so many Israelites and Moab was filled with dread saying, "This horde is going to lick up everything around us!"
So Balak, who was the king of Moab at that time, sent messengers to summon Balaam, the pagan sorcerer, saying: "Come and put a curse on these people because they are too powerful for us. For I know that those you bless are blessed and those you curse are cursed."

"See there," Owl exclaimed, "Balak no doubt believed in the invisible world... so much so that he actually thought to use spiritual warfare rather than physical warfare to defeat Israel."

"Yes, he could see they were out numbered physically," Missfit answered, "The bible says God's

Words are self fulfilling, so when Balaam prophesied what God told him to say, it came true. The same is true today you know Owl, God says in His Word that His Word always accomplishes the purposes for which He sends it." (Isaiah 55:11)

"Anyway...the princes of Moab offered Balaam a lot of money to curse God's people, the Israelites. Balaam told them to stay with him over night while he used divination to ask the Lord, which they did. The bible says God came to Balaam and asked, "Who are these men with you?"

Balaam told God and God said to Balaam, "You must not put a curse on those people, because they are blessed."

The next morning Balaam got up and said to Balak's princes, "Go back to your own country, for the LORD has refused to let me go with you."

So they went back to the King of Moab, but he sent even more princes to Balaam, more numerous and more distinguished than the first group, and they told Balaam, "Don't listen to God, because you will be rewarded handsomely if you'll come with us and put a curse on these people."

But Balaam answered them, "Even if the king gave me his palace filled with silver and gold, I could not do anything great or small to go beyond the command of the LORD."

Balaam was tempted by their offer however, and

rather than simply stating what God had already said, he did a bad thing and went on saying, "Now stay here tonight as the others did, and I will find out what else the LORD will tell me."

"Balaam was hoping God might change His mind and then he'd take their money."

"That night God came to Balaam and said,

"Since these men have come to summon you, go with them, but do only what I tell you."
So Balaam got up in the morning, saddled his donkey and went with the princes of Moab. But knowing that Balaam wanted to curse His people, God was very angry, when he went, and the angel of the LORD stood in the road to oppose him. Balaam was riding on his donkey, and his two servants were with him. When the donkey saw the angel of the LORD standing in the road with a drawn sword in his hand, she turned off the road into a field. Balaam beat her to get her back on the road.

Then the angel of the LORD stood in a narrow path between two vineyards, with walls on both sides. When the donkey saw the angel of the LORD, she pressed close to the wall, crushing Balaam's foot against it. So he beat her again.

Then the angel of the LORD moved on ahead and stood in a narrow place where there was no room to turn, either to the right or to the left. When the donkey saw the angel of the LORD, she lay down under Balaam, and he was angry and beat her with his staff.

Then the LORD opened the donkey's mouth, and she said to Balaam, "What have I done to you to make you beat me these three times?"

Balaam answered the donkey, "You have made a fool of me! If I had a sword in my hand, I would kill you right now."

The donkey said to Balaam, "Am I not your own donkey, which you have always ridden, to this day? Have I been in the habit of doing this to you?" "No," he said.

Then the LORD opened Balaam's eyes, and he saw the angel of the LORD standing in the road with his sword drawn. So he bowed low and fell facedown. The angel of the LORD asked him, "Why have you beaten your donkey these three times? I have come here to oppose you because your path is a reckless one before me. The donkey saw me and turned away from me these three times. If she had not turned away, I would certainly have killed you by now, but I would have spared her."

Balaam said to the angel of the LORD, "I have sinned. I did not realize you were standing in the road to oppose me. Now if you are displeased, I will go back."

The angel of the LORD said to Balaam,
 "Go with the men, but speak only what I tell you."

"You can be sure Balaam went to Moab with renewed courage to obey God after that road trip!

Anyway..."

"When he arrived at Moab, the King went out to greet him asking, "What took you so long?" Balaam said to the King, "Well, I am here now, but I cannot just say anything. I must speak only what God puts in my mouth."

King Balak's anger burned against Balaam and he ordered him to return home, empty handed, which Balaam did, but not before pronouncing another blessing the LORD had told Him to pronounce upon Israel.

God gave Balaam a vision and he saw Jesus off in the distance. God told Balaam to tell what he'd seen.

It's in Numbers 24:17 and Balaam said, "I see him, but not now; I behold him, but not near. A star will come out of Jacob; a scepter will rise out of Israel."

Missfit closed her bible and gave Owl a gentle pat on his head. "Isn't it wonderful?"

Nodding, Owl gasped, "You know what I'm thinking? Because Balaam used dead animals to try and foretell the future, God used an animal to warn Balaam of his!"

Missfit answered, "You are a very wise owl!"

Owl continued, "God is so cool! Thank you for sharing that story with me Missfit. I'd better get back out to the woods now. I've taken up enough of your time."

"Don't mention it," she said while getting up and brushing off her overalls, "It was my pleasure."

They walked together to the fence.

"See you later alligator!" Owl said over his shoulder as he soared up towards the high trees.

"After while crocodile" Missfit echoed to her friend with a grin. Then she picked up her bible and clothes basket and headed back into the house.

Later on this same day, she was out in the back yard again, this time taking the dry laundry off the line, when she saw Clyde coming out of the woods. "Thank you Clyde!" she hollered, "Hound Dog hasn't made a peep since you went out there."

"Any time," Clyde said as he lumbered up to the fence.

Just then Leo the Lion came around from the barn driveway.

"Sure is g-r-r-r-eat to get outside again!" Leo growled.

"Hi Leo," Clyde and Missfit said together.

"What's up?" Clyde asked.

"Have either one of you spoke to Mr. Perkins today?"

"I have," Clyde admitted, "He told me his house is sinking."

"Bummer," Missfit exclaimed, then as if contemplating something, she stopped taking down clothes and walked over to the fence and asked, "What would you guys think about us asking Perkins and Pearly Mae to join the Possum Ranch and move in with you?"

Leo's face furrowed into a frown, "I'd love that, but what if they don't WANT to move?" He went on, "If you remember, they lived out there in your woods long before you built this place."

At that Clyde suggested, "As they say in my family, I think we're getting the cart before the camel! What we need to do is pray about it!"

"That's a good idea Clyde," Said Missfit, "Let's talk to the Lord about it right now....deal?"

"It's a deal" Both animals chimed in unison.

"Abba Father," Missfit began, "Thank You for loving us enough to save us! Thank You that Your Word says in John 15:7 that "If we remain in you and Your Words remain in us, we can ask whatever we wish and it will be given to us." Now I ask that you would make a way for Perkins and Pearly Mae to officially become part of our family, and it's in the mighty name of Jesus we pray, amen."

"And Amen," Clyde and Leo agreed.

Missfit hesitated as she recalled a time when she didn't know God cared about every detail of her life. She thanked Him now that she finally knew the Truths that had set her free.

Chapter 5

Owl Knows a Secret!

"Hoot-Hoot," Came the solemn cry from the tree tops in the now dark woods, and then it came again "Hoot-Hoot!"

"What is that spooky noise?" cried Baby.

"That's just an owl," answered Molly.

"It's very loud," Baby said tearfully, "I'm afraid."

Molly was quick to reassure her, "Don't worry, it can't get in here. The doors are locked."

"What do owls eat?" Baby asked as she crawled up into Molly's lap.

"Fried freckles and whistle-grease," Was heard from behind them, as Merkie entered the barn. Looking around he asked, "Is everyone already in bed?"

Baby and Molly whirled around to see him coming towards them, carrying cookies & milk.

"Merkie, you frightened us!" Molly complained.

"I do most people," he said, as both girls giggled, "Sorry." He added.

"Well… since you have cookies and milk, its ok I guess," Baby assured him.

"I've also got tomorrow's schedule," He said as he poured them each a cup of milk and placed a cookie on a napkin, "Will you make sure the others see it in the morning?"

"Oh goody, where are we going?" Molly squealed, jumping up, nearly causing the Baby puppet to slide down to the floor.

"It says here we're scheduled to set up at 9 a.m. for an Easter Egg Hunt in Fort Wayne, so we'll need to leave by 8:00 a.m."

"We'll make sure everyone knows," Molly assured as she sat Baby in her high chair, adding, "C'mon little one, eat up. We need to get to bed. Tomorrow's going to be a big day!"

Rubbing her eyes Baby added, "Thank you for the snack Merkie."

"You're welcome, 'night all," he answered as he turned to go back to the main house.
Then he heard, "Hoot-Hoot," coming from the woods.

Deciding to pay Owl a quick visit, he headed towards the woods calling, "Hoot-Hoot right back at you…Mr. Owl!"

Owl fluttered down out of his tree and landed right on top of Merkies head!

"What are you trying to do?" Merkie hollered.

"Shush! You'll wake them up!" Owl responded.

"You don't think all that Hooting already did? Besides, wake who up?" Merkie demanded, "And get off of my head!"

"The possums, that's who," Owl whispered from on top of Merkie's hat.

"But its dark out," Merkie whispered, "They should already be up by now."

"I know, usually they would be," Owl explained, "But neither one of them got to sleep today until long after lunch time."

Merkie stood there holding the milk jug in one hand and the cookie plate in the other, with Owl perched on top of his head, and replied, "How do you know so much?"

"I'm an Owl!" the big bird responded, "and I'm very wise", Then bending down and looking at Merkie upside down, right in the face, Owl continued with, "Besides that….I pay attention!"

"Ha!" Merkie laughed, "You call it paying attention? I call it being a very nosey owl."

"I know a secret, I know a secret!" Owl repeated.

"What?" asked Merkie.

"If I told you it wouldn't be a secret anymore now, would it!" Owl said right out loud, forgetting to whisper.

"Would you like some cookies and milk?" Merkie whispered.

"No thanks to the milk, but I'll have a cookie!" Owl replied, as he finally hopped down off of Merkies hat onto his shoulder and then jumped on down to the ground.

Glad to finally be set free, Merkie tossed down a cookie and quickly headed for the house saying," Good Night Owl!"

"Aren't you even curious about my secret?" Owl hollered out.

Merkie was already in the garage, but came to a stop. Turning back around he peered out towards the woods wondering what might have happened today that he didn't know about. "Ok Owl," Merkie gave in, "I'll bite."

Owl stopped crunching on his cookie, walked to the garage and jumping up onto the hood of the car began saying in a whisper," Perkins did something very brave today Merkie!"

"Perkins? What did HE do?" Merkie responded.

"He believed God!" Owl beamed.

"Wow, that's really good!" Merkie exclaimed.

"You know about his sinking house, right?" Owl asked.

"Yes," Merkie said, "I heard he was upset."

Owl went on, "That's right, until good ole Clyde, the best beast of burden there ever was, came over and told him the story about baby Moses being placed in the river by his mother, Jachobed."

Merkie took a seat on his step stool and asked, "Were you there?"
"Close enough," Owl stated, "The trees and the wind carry sounds upwards you know, especially voices, so I heard everything."

"So what happened?" Merkie wondered.

"Perkins made the decision that God was bigger than his problems." Owl choked up,
"He said a prayer and cast all his cares to the Lord, went inside and he's been snoring loud ever since."

Just then the porch lights all came on and Merkie jumped up proclaiming. "Missfit's probably wondering if I'm ever bringing this milk back in!"

"Time for me to go and give a hoot anyway," said Owl with a wink, as he took off in the cool night air.

Merkie stood in the driveway for just one more second, looking up at the star filled sky, and thanked God for His great love for him.

He relayed the entire story he'd just heard from Owl to Missfit while she micro waved them each a cup of hot milk.
She didn't have time to tell Merkie about her and the Camel and Lion praying together earlier. She was tired and it was late.
All she could think about was getting to bed for a good night's sleep, for tomorrow would be a big day!

"Good night," She whispered as her head hit her pillow, "I love you." But Merkie was already asleep.

Chapter 6

Nocturnal Nights

Pearly Mae couldn't believe it when she opened her eyes...it had already gotten dark out! She never slept that long! She began wondering where her friend Perkins was too. He always woke her up long before now, in some form or fashion, either knocking on her house, or just making a ruckus.

She tidied up her place and headed towards his house, just in time to see him coming towards her on the path.
"Howdy Perkins" Pearly Mae smiled, "Fancy meeting you here!"

"Yup, I'm just crazy about walking through these woods." Perkins grinned.

"What's that?" Pearly Mae wondered.

"Ask me how a crazy possum goes through the forest," Perkins insisted.

"Ok," Pearly Mae went along, "Just how does a crazy possum go through the forest?"
Perkins stood up tall declaring, "He takes a Psycho

path!"

"Ha-ha-ha," Pearly Mae howled, "That was a good one Perkins! I'm glad you haven't lost your sense of humor."

"Yes, I'm a new possum!" Perkins sang.

Pearly Mae gasped, "You got your house fixed!"

"Nope, not yet" He admitted, "But I'm not going to worry 'bout my house anymore. I'm going to focus instead on my great big God."

"What happened?" She inquired further.

"Well, it all began with you Pearly Mae!" Perkins went on, "Yesterday when you stopped by, you said something I couldn't forget."

"I did?" Pearly Mae backed up.
"I had just complained about not being able to see Jesus, remember, and you said I should fix my eyes on what I can't see because those things we can't see are eternal?" Perkins reminded her.

"Yes, I remember," Pearly Mae said, as she took a seat on a tree stump.

"But I didn't do it," Perkins went on, "I kept focusing on my sinking house. All day long my problem grew and grew in my mind until it became as big as an elephant! You may think I really AM crazy but I actually fought that elephant Pearly Mae! And it wasn't a nice elephant!"

"I seem to recall telling you that whatever you focused on would become bigger and bigger." Pearly Mae smiled.

"You weren't kidding!" Perkins continued, "Then Clyde Camel stopped by and told me how Jochabed believed God so much that she actually floated her darling baby boy Moses in a basket down the Nile River. Do you know that because she so totally entrusted her problem into God's care and keeping, He rewarded her?"
"I've read the story, yes," Pearly Mae choked up, "Thanks to Merkie and Missfit.
They gave me a bible when I first met them. Missfit said she'd been taught things about God and the Bible her whole life but when she began reading it for herself she realized most of what she'd been told wasn't true. That got me to thinking, so I spend time every day now reading it for myself too."

"They gave me a bible too, but I guess you already know, I never did read it," Perkins admitted. "But all that's going to change 'cause I decided yesterday to trust the unseen hand of God with all of my worries!"

"Perkins! That's wonderful!" Pearly Mae cheered, "You are one awesome possum!"

Perkins dropped his head stating, "Awe chucks, I'm not either, but you shore are."

Last one to the mud hole is a rotten egg!" Pearly Mae squealed, as she took off running deeper into the dark woods.

48

Perkins shouted, "If yawl ask me, that mud hole smells like rotten eggs" as he easily passed her up arriving first at the murky mud hole.

Standing on the edge, Perkins looked intently at the water.

"Shoo! Pearly Mae exclaimed as she arrived, "I think I've gained a pound or two over the winter! That little run just 'bout finished me off!"

"Shush" Perkins whispered, "Listen!"

Pearly Mae leaned against a big rock and listened....and listened....and listened...."Shore is quiet out here in these here woods, isn't it!" She panted.

"Croak-croak," Was the familiar sound Perkins had been listening for.

"There it is!" He exclaimed, "A sure sign winter is over! Hello Frog Friends!" Perkins squealed with glee.

Just then a mother deer and her baby came walking down the pathway together. The entire path through the woods had actually been made by the many deer that pass through every day.
Two small rabbits scurried from tree to tree, stopping to nibble something occasionally.
The neighborhood raccoon nosed his way up towards the house to look for food, as did a really huge stray Siamese cat, which set off the motion detector lights Merkie had installed.

"Ding dong ding dong" it chimed as all the lights flooded on. Every creature in the woods ran for shelter, except the possums. They just laughed as they watched every one else vacate the premises.

"I'm hungry," Perkins said, "How about you?"

"Yes" Pearly Mae replied, "I'm famished!"

"I'd be plum honored if you'd join me for an insect hunt," Perkins offered.

"Why Perkins, I'd love to!" Pearly Mae answered as she locked arms with him.

After finding all the insects they wanted, Perkins invited her to his house and the two of them worked together in the kitchen frying them into tacos, which they totally devoured.
   Looking around at Perkins house, Pearly Mae decided not to bring up the topic of his cracking walls, but he did.
"I'm going to wait and see what God does." He said.

"What God does about what?" Pearly Mae feigned.

"You know...my sinking house!" He answered.
"Now, what do you say we have a sing along?"

"Count me in!" She answered, standing up.
Both Possums sang at the top of their lungs and danced every dance they knew until the sun came up.

50

Meanwhile, Merkie and Missfit and the many puppets and critters who all live on the Possum Ranch lay sound asleep, totally unaware of all the activity happening right there in their own woods.

And because they'd set their trust and love on Him, God sent His angels to watch over them.   (Psalm 91:14-16)

Chapter 7

The Egg Hunt

Missfit tried to be quiet as she made her way downstairs to start the coffee, but Merkie stirred, "Good morning."

"Good morning, how'd you sleep?" She asked.

"Mostly on my side," Merkie answered in his usual jovial manner. He began making the bed as Missfit disappeared down the stairs.

Once coffee was on, she went to her desk and checked the phone messages and began writing about the previous days activities in her journal. After giving the care of the entire day into God's hands in a prayer and reading several chapters from His Word, it was off to the kitchen to make breakfast.

By now Merkie was downstairs too, making toast as Missfit whipped up scrambled eggs.
With the kitchen all cleaned up, it was time to head for the showers and then to the basement where their dressing room is. Merkie was ready first, (as usual) so he went on out to the barn to start up their big truck.
Unlocking the barn door, he stepped inside where

52

there was a hub of activity. All of the puppets and critters were attending to their chores and necessary tasks for the day.

"Good morning Merkie!" Priscilla cried gleefully.

"Well good morning Pris," Merkie laughed, "You're up before breakfast today!"

"Yes," She proudly answered, "And we're ready to roll." She whistled, and held the truck door open as all of the Possum Ranch family marched in and took their places inside.

Merkie opened the huge garage door and backed their big yellow clown truck out into the drive, where he turned around and headed for the main house to pick Missfit up.

"Did you remember to bring water?" She asked as she climbed in.

"Yup," Merkie answered, "I may be slow, but I sure don't get much done."
"You're such a clown Merkie!" She said affectionately as they pulled out of their driveway, then something caught her eye as they passed by the woods. She strained to see what it was, but all she saw were the two Possum's houses sitting there in silence. No one was around, so she assumed they must already be asleep for the day.

"I sure wish the possums were going with us," she dreamed, "I mean, we do call ourselves the Possum Ranch Puppets and Clowns!"

"Have you ever invited them?" Merkie asked.

"No," Missfit admitted, "Only because they sleep during the day. Do you think it'd be worth a try to at least ask them to come along just once?"

"I think that right now, with Perkins house sinking and all, he might be downright glad to not only join our little family, but to move on in with the rest of the critters," Merkie smiled, "And then we'd have our very own Possums!"

"Let's ask them both tonight," Missfit suggested excitedly, "When we return."

"Sounds like a good plan!" Merkie beamed.

After about an hour of driving, Merkie stopped for gas, which caused quite a stir at the station. People just aren't accustomed to seeing two clowns, out in big yellow trucks.

When they arrived at the Easter Egg Hunt, the eggs were still being hidden by several fun loving adults.

Everybody in the Ranch family working together made it possible to get the entire puppet stage and sound system set up in just 30 minutes.

Before you could say "Jack Rabbit" there must have been 200 children outside on the church lawn searching for eggs! And the prizes were great! Bicycles, basketballs, skate boards, and lots of candy had been purchased by the church's members to be given away.

54

Afterwards, everyone came inside to retrieve their prizes, but first, they were treated to the Possum Ranch Puppet and Clown show.

Merkie and Missfit were introduced and they truly started out with a BANG, as Merkie proceeded to burst a balloon right off the bat! Then he did one of his magic tricks.
Two of the glow puppets dressed up like angels and did a skit for everyone about Palm Sunday.

Missfit explained, "You know, Palm Sunday was the day Jesus rode into Jerusalem on a donkey just as the Bible predicted. (Zechariah 9:9)
The people laid palm branches down along the road before him.
The most amazing thing is that the exact day it would happen had been foretold in the book of Daniel. (Daniel 9:25)
That's why Jesus said if the people were to stop shouting praises to "God in the Highest" that the very stones would cry out.
(Luke 19:40)
God's long awaited Messiah was revealed at last, and it happened on the very day the Bible had predicted it would."

After Missfit told the story she had eight people from the audience dance while wearing funny hats and glasses and the puppets sang. To finish, Merkie and Missfit led hand motions to a song titled, "Supernatural" praising their great Supernatural God.

They stood at the door and passed out Scripture

Coins to everyone as they left, wishing them all a great big God Bless You, before tearing down the stage and loading it all back up into the truck to head home.

Bum pity-bump down the road they went. Missfit just started to doze off when she heard little voices chanting from their bunks...
"Give me a P, and give me an-I, give me a z-z-a!
Give me a P, and give me an-I, give me a z-z-a!"

Looking over at Merkie she said, "Do you think someone is hinting for pizza?"

It suddenly became quiet, so Merkie said, "I've got an idea! Why don't we call and order a pizza!"

"My goodness Merkie," Missfit played along, "What a good idea!" she said as she flipped open her cell phone and hit the speed dial for their favorite pizza place. After ordering 5 large pizzas to go, she said into her phone, "And by the way, we are the clowns, so if there's anyone there who doesn't like clowns, I just wanted to warn you that we're coming."

By the time they rolled in to the pizza place, their order was ready and everyone inside was all smiles when they saw them pulling in.

Once at home, everyone gathered in the barn's dining area. Merkie prayed and thanked God for the awesome privilege of sharing His great love with the good people in Ft. Wayne.

Everyone thanked God for their supper, and the pizza was enjoyed by all.

They visited awhile and enjoyed talking about all of the different things they'd seen and done all day before Missfit spoke up saying, "I'm gonna have to end this party I'm afraid, because we have a date with a couple of possums."

"Oh-oh, are they in trouble?" Vern the Bird blurted. "Don't be a bird brain Vern" Merkie said with a wink, "No, they are not in trouble."

"We just want to talk to them about joining our Possum Ranch family," Missfit confided.

At that, all the puppets stared wide eyed and you could have heard a pin drop, except for Clyde and Leo, and they gave each other a wink.

"See you tomorrow!" Merkie said, as he closed the barn door behind him.

He and Missfit headed towards the woods, while saying a prayer for God to grant them favor in the eyes of their possum friends.

Chapter 8

A Possum Invitation

"Whose house should we go to first Merkie?" Missfit asked as they walked together from the barn up towards the house.

"Ours I think," he replied.

"I meant, which one of the possum's houses?" she sighed.

"It doesn't matter to me," Merkie stated emphatically, "but first we need to stop up at our house…to get a flashlight. It may still be light out right now but it's not going to last long."

"Gotcha," She said as she sat down on the front porch rocking chair and began rocking, "I'll wait here".

Merkie came back out onto the porch holding their camping lantern, "This will be better yet!"

They both walked around back towards where the path going into the woods begins, and as they did, they were delighted to see that Hound Dog was outside of his dog house.

Missfit laughed right outloud when she noticed that he was wearing a tie!

"Woof!" He barked, "Good evening! To what do I owe this honor?"

"Good timing no doubt," Merkie said, "What's up with the tie?"

"You noticed!" Hound Dog beamed, "I just gave myself a promotion!"

"You look very nice Hound Dog," Missfit complimented.

"Thank you! I decided it was time for me to quit being the Underdog and start being the Top Dog!"

Merkie and Missfit looked at each other in surprise at Hound Dogs words.
"But Hound Dog," Missfit started, "Don't you know you're already like one of the family?"

"Really, which one of you do I take after?" Hound Dog grinned big.

"Well…Merkie has a wet nose like yours!" she answered.

"I do?" Merkie said trying to look down at his big red nose.

"Just go along with me," Missfit whispered as she poked him in the ribs.

"Yes! Sometimes I do!" Merkie agreed as he straightened up, "And we really need your help right now!"

"We do?" Missfit was quick to respond.

"We do!" Merkie said, raising his eyebrows at her.

"Of course we do….to do what again Merkie?" she questioned.

"To escort us into the woods to visit the possums," Merkie replied.

"Oh yes! You can be our police dog," Missfit exclaimed, "Won't you please?"

"Why yes, in fact, I've always wanted to be a police dog," Hound Dog said overjoyed.
Merkie stepped back and eyed the hound dog saying, "You don't look like any police dog I've ever seen!"

60

"Of course not," Hound Dog reasoned, "I'm in the secret service."

Merkie and Missfit looked at one another again and then busted out laughing, "C'mon" Merkie commanded with a smirk, as he opened the gate to the kennel.

Hound Dog wanted to jump up and lick Merkie's face he was so happy, but he controlled himself because Hound Dog is really a good dog!
The three of them headed off towards the woods together to pay the possums a visit.
Hound Dog ran ahead to Perkins house first and began sniffing all around it. "Yip yup," he said, "He's in there!"

Merkie gave a knock on the roof and Perkins came right out.

"Howdy yawl," he began, "Why it sure is plum fine good to see yawl!"

"It's good to see you too Perkins," Missfit remarked.

"I hope we didn't wake you," Said Merkie.

"Nope," Perkins responded, "Been up bout' half an hour. Kin I get yawl some coffee?"

"No thank you," Missfit answered, "It keeps me awake."

"I'd love some," Merkie responded.

"Me too!" chimed Hound Dog, "with cream."

Perkins went back inside for coffee.
Just then Pearly Mae came out of her house and saw Perkins guests, so she scurried across the path to join them.

"My-my Hound Dog, you shore do look pretty in that tie," Pearly Mae sweetly said.
    "Thanks!" Hound Dog beamed again.

"He's been promoted into the secret service," Missfit said with a wink.

"Ah, a celebrity, huh," Pearly Mae feigned, also with a wink, "I always knew you had it in you Hound Dog!"

Perkins came out carrying a tray of coffee and upon seeing Pearly Mae said, "Coffee?"

"Yes, thanks Perkins."

He went back in and came back with a cup for Pearly Mae too.

Missfit dug some mints out of her pocket and sharing one with each of her friends, she began the conversation, "We sure had a fun time today!"
"What'd you do?" Perkins asked.

"We entertained for an Easter Egg hunt, in Ft. Wayne," she answered.

"What all do you do?" Perkins asked.
"I did some cool magic tricks!" Merkie proudly proclaimed.

"And I tried to…." Missfit's voice trailed off, "But it didn't go well, as usual."

"She says I distract her," Merkie confessed, "I told her that's what I was best in at school, addition and distraction!"

The two Possums, Missfit, and Hound Dog all howled at Merkies play on words!

"The puppets did a skit too," Merkie continued, "and Missfit sang a song while some of the audience did a dance, wearing big goofy sunglasses and hats."

"Did you tell them any good jokes?" Perkins pondered.

"Actually, that's why we're here Perkins," Merkie said. "No one knows more jokes than you do, and well, we were wondering if you'd consider joining our Possum Ranch Family."

Looking at Pearly Mae, Missfit added, "And you too Pearly Mae! We've been calling ourselves the Possum Ranch Puppets and Clowns but frankly, we need some Possums!"

"We'd love it if you both would consider joining us!" Merkie hoped.

"I'll be horns waggled!" Perkins stammered, "Here I am with a sinking house, and just one day after trusting the entire problem to the Lord, this happens! Isn't God good? Do you have room for us… for real?"

"I know you both sleep during the day, so I realize you wouldn't get any rest in the bunk house. But I'm prepared to make you each a place of your own in our two smaller barns."

Perkins contemplated, "Thank You Jesus!" He shouted up to the sky with a big toothy grin.

"What would my function include?" asked Pearly Mae.

"Well, Hound Dog does a great job of watching over the place during the day. But you both could keep an eye on things at night." Missfit answered, "And all the puppets love you so much Pearly Mae, I know you'd be a tremendous help as we travel, just caring for the little ones would help me a lot. Then, if you feel comfortable with it, you could even perform with us, if you'd like!"

"When do we start?" She said, marveling at the possibilities that lie ahead.

"Since tomorrow is Easter Sunday, how about joining us for dinner, or would supper work better, or would you prefer breakfast?" Merkie stammered, realizing they'd be asleep all day.

"Land sakes Merkie, I don't want to be a bother," Perkins drawled. "Just tell me what time you're eating and I'll notify the rooster."

Missfit reasoned, "Church is out by 11:00 a.m., so dinner should be ready by 12:30 p.m. without too much difficulty."
"It's a date then," Pearly Mae enthusiastically proclaimed adding, "If you'll come over and wake me Perkins. I don't always hear the rooster."

"I'll be there with bells on girl!" He promised.
"Oh boy," said Hound Dog from Missfits lap, "That means there's going to be table scraps! I love Sunday dinner table scraps!"

Missfit had been sitting on a tree stump but now stood up holding Hound Dog, telling him and Merkie, "I'm a little sleepy. Are you two ready to say goodnight?"

"I am" Merkie grinned, "I haven't slept for days!"

"Whoa! I bet you're really tired!" Hound Dog remarked.

"Not in the least!" Merkie said yawning, "I sleep nights."

"Tee-he," Perkins laughed.

Pearly Mae said, "He got cha' on that one Dog."
       Perkins jumped in with, "Do you go to sleep on your right side or on your left side?"

To which Merkie responded, "My right side."

"Really," Perkins joked, "That's funny; all of me goes to sleep at once!"

"Good one Perkins," Merkie laughed again.

"C'mon granny, it's past my bed time," He said taking Missfit's hand.

"Lead the way my love, you've got the light." She yawned.

"Good night or I mean good morning, or whatever it is to you Possums," Hound Dog stammered.

"Back at you," Perkins smiled; he then picked up the empty coffee cups, and thought to himself, "I'm sure going to tell Clyde the Camel thank you for telling me that story about Jachobed trusting baby Moses to God."

"I'll wash those cups," Pearly Mae demanded as she waddled into Perkins house behind him.

Once Hound Dog was securely in his kennel, Merkie and Missfit went inside and got ready for bed, thanking the Lord for giving them another blessed day.
Both clowns remembered well a time when their lives were empty and meaningless, but today they are full to the brim and running over!

Chapter 9

Disarmed and Defeated!

Sunday morning always means pecan pancakes on
the Possum Ranch!
Granny cooks breakfast all week long for the puppet
people in the bunk house, so Harley graciously
volunteered to do it on Sundays.
Pecan pancakes are his specialty, and naturally
everyone looks forward to it!

But this particular Sunday morning, when Harley
came out of the bunk house into the dining area, he
couldn't find anyone.
"You who, Where is everyone?" He hollered as he
searched.
"Hello! It's Sunday, this is the pancake man...." He
sang joyfully, but with no response.
He thought to himself, "This is strange."

Then, suddenly he heard a slow deep,
"Hello!" Harley's heart nearly stopped at the evil
sounding voice.

Spinning around to look, he cried out, "Whoa! It's a
snake!"
The snake raised his head up and Harley thought for
sure he was going to faint!
"Take it easy man," Came the snakes reply, "I'm
cool."
68

Harley found himself running backwards until he could go no further.

"M-m-m-m-my name's H-H-Harley." He said, reaching his trembling hand as if to shake. Embarrassed at how silly that was…you know, since snakes don't have hands, Harley immediately pulled his hand back gasping, "Sorry."

"I'm pleased to meet you Harley," Responded the snake in his raspy voice.

"But I'm afraid I sent your family running too. It's ok though, every one reacts to me like that. I think it has something to do with one of my ancestor's way back in the Garden of Eden."

Harley found himself actually feeling sympathy for the snake and risked saying, "That wasn't your fault."

Lowering his head the snake contended, "It's ok, I know."

"Say, I've always wondered about something," Harley risked further.

"What's that?" asked the snake.

Walking up just a bit closer to him Harley dared, "Did your ancestors ever have legs?"

"How would I know?" The snake flinched.

"Didn't your parents ever talk about it?" Harley inquired.

"I'm a snake," He said, jolting forward.

"Hey," Harley reasoned, "The snake in the

Garden of Eden talked, and you're talking to me right now."

The snake looked around for a minute and then said in a much friendlier tone, "Oh alright. You see, I'm actually an undercover agent for the King of Kings."

Harley's eyes got so big they nearly popped out of their sockets, as he declared, "Whoa, no way!"

"Yes way," answered the snake calmly. "And the truth is that it's quite appropriate that the devil is represented in the bible by a
serpent, because we don't have arms, legs, or even feet."

Harley swallowed hard and asked, "And why is that so appropriate?"

"Because the bible says the devil has been disarmed and defeated....by Jesus, the King of Kings!" He announced boldly.

Harley relaxed a bit as he thought about it, then said, "You mean like, DIS-ARMED and DE-FEETED? Wow! That's a good one! Ha! That surely does put him at a disadvantage!"

The Snake grinned big saying, "You can bet it makes him a little disagreeable too!"

By now Harley was really warming up to the snake and said, "Ha! That's what he gets for being so dishonest!"

The snake totally agreed, "John 10:10 says the devil is completely devoted to, killing, stealing and destroying humans, making their lives seem like a roller coaster! That's why my advice to them is; Trust God....and try to eat a light lunch!"

"Hey, I've discovered & determined, you're a lot of fun, for a disarmed & defeated snake!" Harley cheered.

"I like you too Harley," came the Snakes reply, "So I'm going to let you in on a little known kingdom secret."

"Hit me!" Harley said, pulling up a chair.

The snake looked around again, as if he were concerned some one may be listening, but went on, "Jesus defeated and disarmed the devil when He took onto Himself the curse Adam & Eve caused. But you'll notice I still have a mouth," Then wagging his tail he added, "And a tail."

Harleys gaze was fixed onto the snake now, as he said, "Oh, I surely do see that!"

"Good," shared the snake, "And that's why it's so important to pay attention to every detail written in the Word of God!"

Harley thought for a second before declaring, "I hate to tell you, but that's no secret."

"Allow me to finish," Said the Snake as he continued

slowly wagging his big strong tail. "Few people realize that because Satan is a defeated foe, all he's able to do is to make improper suggestions and intimidate, through misleading thoughts, because he has no other weapon. But born again believers in Jesus DO have a weapon!"

"They do?" asked a very interested Harley.

"They sure do," the snake answered, "The Word of God is a mighty weapon that sets people free from the power of the dominion of darkness, as the Holy Spirit guides them into the truth."

"Ok Mr. Snake, I'll buy that," Harley analyzed "but what's that got to do with your tail?"

"It's written in the weapon! In the first book of Timothy, the 4th chapter it says, "The Spirit clearly says that in later times some will abandon the faith and follow deceiving spirits and things taught by demons. So people should have nothing to do with such myths and old wives tales."

Harley was surprised to hear the snake quoting scripture and exclaimed, "Wow!
The devil deceives people with false tales?"
"Yup!" declared the snake, still wagging his tail, "In their thoughts, so... the only tales you should believe, are the details found in God's Word!"

Harley sat up straight at the realization of what Snake said and proclaimed, "So it's all about what we believe is true?"

"Yup," Said the snake, "And because the enemy's name means accuser all he does day and night is condemn and accuse people in their thoughts!"

"Hmmm" Harley pondered, "So when I start thinking no one likes me or I can't do anything good enough, that's the devil lying to me?"

The snake stopped wagging his tail and raised his head up proclaiming, "That's a fact Jack!"

Harley interrupted, "Hey, I remember hearing something about God's people actually overcoming the accuser by the blood of the Lamb, and the WORD of their testimony! I think it's in the book of Revelation."

"Very good Harley" exclaimed the snake. "My boss, King Jesus, sent His Holy Spirit to the earth to enable people to think like God thinks. Then when the devil tells them a lie, all they have to do is say, "It is written…"

"Just like Jesus did," Harley calmed, "when the devil tried to tempt Him." (Matthew 4:4)

Before he could respond, the snake looked up and saw what looked like an entire wall coming down on him, shouting, "EGADS" he quickly scrambled out of the way just in time as it came down with a loud crash.

"Yikes" Harley jumped off of his chair and picking it up, he held it in front of him like a shield. Then he figured that all of the puppets must have run and hid behind one of the puppet stage walls when they'd first seen the snake.

He began to laugh to himself thinking "If they don't look silly!"
Every one of them was on top of the other with the stage wall now laying flat beneath them on the barn floor.

"I've got to report for duty now," the snake said and he slithered out of sight.
"Wait, don't go, I didn't get your name," Harley cried, as he ran to the spot where the snake disappeared. Seeing all the puppets' eyes on him he ordered, "Go get him!"

The puppets all scurried to regain their composure and earnestly pretended to be searching for the snake, but secretly hoping they'd never see it again.

After a few minutes Harley looked at his watch and remembering the pancakes proclaimed, "Never mind him, lets eat!"

"Yay" Was their happy reply as they all found a place at the table.
It wasn't long until Harley had the grill covered in circles of pancake batter.

"Can I add the pecans?" asked the pink little girl puppet known as Pinky.

"I guess so, but be careful, the grill is hot," Harley

commanded in a fatherly tone.

Just then the side door popped open and in walked Merkie looking his Sunday best.

He was carrying a grocery sack full of different flavored pancake syrups and a pound of butter. "Missfit said you'd need this," he announced.

"Thanks Merkie," replied the excited puppets.

"Come and join us," Begged Pinky as she whirled around to face him.

"Thanks, but no thanks," Merkie resisted. "But remember, we're all having Sunday dinner together today at 12:30."

"Yippee!" Pinky cheered, while all the others joined her.

"Yippee...we love Sundays," They all cheered together.

"Me too," Merkie said, "Mostly because Missfit and I get to go to church, which is where we're headed right now. I'll ring the dinner bell though, when it's time for you all to come up to the house, ok?"

"Thanks Merkie," Harley took the syrup and butter from him saying, "Eat up everyone, your pancakes are on the table."

Looking back at their plates the puppets saw they'd been filled with steaming hot pecan pancakes.

Grandpa puppet announced, "Take each others hands and let's pray."

Merkie smiled big and closed the door behind him, thanking God himself for another new day of life.

God rewarded his gratitude and came to him during the praise and worship that morning and spoke into his heart. He told Merkie in his spirit how He loved him with an everlasting love and that He'd never ever leave nor forsake him.

Chapter 10

Sunday Dinner

"Ok Merkie," Missfit directed, "You can ring the dinner bell now."

Merkie stepped out onto the front porch to where he'd hung the Stainless Steel bell he'd hand made himself, for Missfit. Thankful it was still too early for the wasps to be living in it, he grabbed the ringer and rang it for the puppet people...Ding dong -ding dong -ding dong!

"You rang?" Merkie heard Pearly Mae Possum say behind him. When he turned he saw her and Perkins both coming up the sidewalk.

"Come inside friends! And Happy Easter," He said opening the door wide.

"Missfit, look who's here," He announced happily as they entered the family room, "It's the possum pair!"

"Happy Easter, it's so good to see you," she replied. Just then the door bell rang.

"C'mon in" Merkie hollered as he was setting up the last folding table.

Harley held the door, while what seemed to Perkins like fifty puppet people of all different shapes and sizes, came marching in.

"Mmmm" exclaimed Molly, "something smells good enough to eat. Can I help?"

"Thank you," Missfit answered while handing her a bright yellow table cloth, "You could put this on that last table for me."

Harley hurried to help Molly shake out the cloth and unfold it over the table saying, "You can all be seated now."

Pearly Mae scurried to Perkins side to watch the parade as each puppet took their place. Perkins thought it looked like everyone already knew exactly where to sit.
"How do you want to do this Missfit?" Asked Merkie, guiding Perkins and Pearly Mae to the table covered with a bright red cloth.

Rusty offered, "They can sit next to me!"
"Why thank you, we will," Both possums replied with gratitude.

Pointing to the counter tops, Missfit said, "The silverware is there, the drinks are here, and the food is over there, and... the red table gets to go first."

"YAY," The puppets cheered.

"After prayer," Grandpa assured.

Everyone bowed their heads and Merkie began, "Lord, thank You for this day of life, this food we're about to eat, and for everyone here today. Thank You for sending Jesus to enable us not only to have a blessed life right now, but eternal life forever, and it's in His mighty name that we lean, rely, confidently trust and pray, amen."

"AMEN!" Everyone chimed in.

The red table group lined up to fill their plates and Missfit added, "Yellow can go second, blue is third, green is forth, purple is fifth and then orange." Then she and Merkie took their places at the orange table.
Perkins gave Pearly Mae a nudge as he was in line behind her, whispering, "We're the only animals here!"

"I noticed that too," she responded rather nervously, "I wonder where the rest of them are."

"We saw Hound Dog in his Kennel on our way, remember?" Perkins whispered.

Overhearing them, Butch butted in, "Oh they already ate and now they're out in the barn setting up to entertain us during dessert."

"Cool!" Perkins nodded, thinking to himself what a great day this was!

All the tables had been called and everyone had filled their plates before Merkie tapped on his water glass with his dinner knife.

"I want to propose a toast...to the newest members of the Possum Ranch puppets and clowns....Perkins and Pearly Mae Possum!"

"CHEERS!" Everyone said, raising their glasses.

"And welcome to our family," said Missfit, "You both are an answer to our prayers!"
By the time the last table was cleared and the kitchen cleaned, the animals in the barn were ready and waiting.

"Here they come now," Shouted Vern the bird from the open barn door. Flying over to the microphone, Verne announced, "Welcome to the Possum Ranch Critters barn dance and dessert bar!"

The puppets bunk house is actually a big yellow box truck that's been converted into an RV. Merkie had backed it out of the barn earlier so there was plenty of room to party.

"Find yourself a seat, or feel free to dance along with the music." Vern continued, "First off, I'm happy to introduce you to my favorite girl in the world, Wildthing. Come on up here honey."
Every one applauded, except Perkins and Pearly Mae.

They were sitting on Clyde the camels hump and both of them gasped as they watched Wildthing walk up to the microphone.

"What is she?" Pearly Mae whispered to Clyde.

"I don't know, but I hear she's the spitting image of her father."

At that Perkins laughed, "Oh well, let's hope she's healthy at least."

Shoving him playfully Pearly Mae commanded, "Shush! I think she's going to sing."

Wildthing cleared her throat, turned her back to Vern, and said into the microphone, "I refuse to sing with Vern."

Vern was obviously deeply offended and appeared to be shaken by her sudden obvious rejection.

Turning to the critter band behind him Vern ordered, "Hit it!"

They began to play, and Vern began to sing:
Why do you build me up...Buttercup, baby, just to let me down...and mess me around?"

Wildthing grabbed the microphone out of Verns claws and screeched:
"Because worst of all...you never call lately when you say you will!"

Vern crooned: "But I love you still!"

Wildthing responded: "I need you...bout as much as a toothache, a migraine or trip to Wal-Mart!"

Vern sang:
"Build me up...Buttercup...don't break my heart!"

Wildthing complained:
"I'll be over at ten you told me time and again...but you're late...I wait around and then...
I went to the door...I can't take anymore, it's not you...you let me down again!"

Vern sang hopefully: "Baby baby...try to find...a little time...and I'll make you happy..."

Wildthing bluntly sang:
"I'm just fine... and you're out of your mind if you think I'm crying for you!"

Vern cried: "Boo-who, boo-who
Why do you build me up...Buttercup, baby, just to let me down...and mess me around!"
Wildthing sang back again with: "Because worst of all...you never call lately when you say you will..."
Vern sang boldly: "But I love you still!"

Wildthing sang sarcastically: "I need you...bout

82

as much as a flat tire, a dead phone or trip to Wal-Mart!"

Vern begged: "Build me up...Buttercup...don't break my heart!"

Then Wildthing sang: "To you I'm a toy."

Vern pleaded: "But I could be the boy you adore...If you'd just let me know..."

Wildthing complained: "You're always untrue!"

Vern confessed: "I'm attracted to you...all the more...Why do I need you so? Baby-baby...try to find...a little time...and I'll make you happy..."

Wildthing sang angrily:
"Your elevator, don't go all the way, up to the top! Bop Shoo Bop... ooh - woo..."

Vern begged some more:
"Why do you build me up...Buttercup, baby, just to let me down...and mess me around?"

Wildthing again ridiculed:
"Because worst of all...you never call lately when you say you will..."

Vern bowed low singing: "But I love you still!"

Wildthing heartlessly sang:
"I need you...to be gone or just leave, take a hike and forever depart!"

But Vern just kept singing: "Build me up...Buttercup...
don't break my heart!"

On a roll, Wildthing sang: "I- I-I think you're a few...
feathers short of a whole duck, your slinky's been
kinked from start!"

Sheepishly, Vern whispered back: "Build me up...
Buttercup...Don't break my heart."

Everyone in the place clapped and cheered wildly,
not realizing this had not been a planned comedy
act.

Shocked to see them laughing, Wildthing slapped
Vern across the face, ran to the clown truck, jumped
up onto the running board and leaped in head first,
through the open window.

At that, Leo the Lion couldn't hold it back any more
and let out a great big, "ROAR," In the direction of
Verne, by now a very unhappy and love sick bird.

"What a doe-doe bird!" Moe the Orangutan teased.
"Vern, your mommy must have been a weight lifter!"
"Why would you say that?" Vern sighed.

"That would explain how she raised such a
dumbbell," Moe insulted.

Now everyone was trying not to laugh, but
Pearly Mae's heart was a tender one, and she felt
compassion for Vern, saying, "I know exactly what
your problem is Vern."

"So do I," Vern confessed, "My girlfriend hates me!"

"But would you like to know why?" Pearly Mae continued.

"I'm not sure," Vern confided.

Understanding, she said, "If and when you do want to know, just ask and I'll share a secret of the universe with you."

"Egad" squealed Vern, "The whole universe knows why Wildthing hates my guts? I guess it's time that I know too!"
"Ok, I'll tell you," Pearly Mae began as everyone looked for a place to sit. Everyone except Vern that is, he just stood there. He was so distraught he forgot to stop speaking into the microphone, so every word he said boomed out through the loud speakers.

Wildthing was still hiding in the passenger seat of the truck parked in the driveway, but she could easily hear everything through the open window.

"You apparently are not aware of the spiritual law of sowing and reaping that rules the universe Vern," Pearly Mae noted. "It goes like this: Whatever you sow, that and that only is what you will reap." (Galatians 6:7)
Go on please..." Vern humbly pleaded.

"You are reaping Wildthing's anger because you sowed seeds of distrust by not keeping your promises to her."

"If this is such a secret, how is it that you know about it?" Vern asked.

"Didn't Missfit give you a bible?" she asked.
"Yeah...I've got one...somewhere." Vern admitted.

"It's found in Galatians 6:7-8." She obliged.

"Who's ready for dessert?" Granny announced, and everyone said they were!
Everyone that is, except the Possums. They excused themselves and each one went to their own house in the woods to retire for the remainder of the day.

"We're so very glad you're going to join us," everyone shared as they gave hugs and hand shakes at the door.

"So are we," Pearly Mae promptly replied.

"Thank you for dinner and a wonderful time," Perkins added, as he let Pearly Mae walk ahead of him, as a real gentleman always does.

"We love you," Missfit hollered from the open barn door, as she watched them waddle up the walk.

Perkins stopped in his tracks when he heard her, and turning around said, "Yawl can't know how much you have come to mean to us!"

Pearly Mae stopped also, "Good day" she hollered, and then they both turned and went towards the woods.

Missfit silently thanked God in her heart for answering her prayer concerning the possums, thinking, "Now we truly are a Possum Ranch!"

Remembering a time when all she knew was pain, she thanked God all day in her heart for the peace of mind that is hers because of what Jesus did 2000 years ago.

God took note of her gratitude and sent so many happy thoughts into her mind that she literally giggled all day long.

That's what knowing that we've been made right with God does you know!
(2 Corinthians 5:21)
It allows us to enter into His undisturbed peace and well being because our confidence is in Jesus and NOT in our own righteousness.
Trusting in Jesus rather than your own pitiful righteousness can and will heal you everywhere you hurt! (Luke 8:48)

Chapter 11

Campfire Story

Everyone enjoyed Granny puppet's homemade vanilla ice cream while listening to the "Critter Puppet Band" playing one great tune after another all afternoon long.

The people puppets took turns singing and dancing with each other until Leo Lion noticed it was supper time.
"My stomach is growling!" He complained.

Negative Ned the Rooster came back with, "Is there any part of you that doesn't growl?"

"Let's build a bonfire," Pleaded Rusty, ignoring the roosters' rude comment to Leo.

Merkie was happy to oblige him, grabbing some newspaper from the stack kept just for that purpose. Inside the fenced in back yard is a fire ring Merkie built himself out of steel and bricks.
"Hey! I think I've got some hot dogs in the freezer we can roast!" Missfit called as she headed towards the house, "Come on everybody."

Each puppet grabbed a lawn chair and headed for the opened gate, as Merkie lit the fire.

They sang several rounds of "Row-Row- Row Your Boat" and "Jesus Loves the Little Children" before the fire was burning well enough to roast hot dogs, which they all did for each other, and marshmallows too.

Then Missfit asked, "Who wants to hear a story?"

"Me! ...I do!" They all agreed.

"Tell us the Easter Story!" Giggles begged.

"Ok," Missfit began, "Matthew 27:45-46 says, "While Jesus hung on the cross, darkness came over all the land from the sixth hour until the ninth hour. About the ninth hour Jesus cried out in a loud voice, "My God, my God, why have you forsaken me?" Grandpa interrupted, "Jesus was quoting the 22nd Psalm, which was written hundreds of years earlier! Yet when you read it you see He was dropping hints because it's also a list of clues that point to the fact that He truly was their promised savior, and even describes His crucifixion in detail."

"Did daylight return then?" Butch asked, holding his feet closer to the warm fire.

"Yes," Missfit continued, "But there also was an earth quake, and the curtain inside the Holiest part of the temple was torn in two from the top to the bottom, showing the world once and for all that it was God Himself who initiated and authorized not only access into His presence, but also the promise of supernatural and heaven born possibilities now coming into each and every believers life, whether Jew or Gentile.

You see, it was no ordinary curtain, but such a heavy woven fabric that it couldn't even be cut, almost like a metal mesh. Hebrews 10:20 says that curtain represents Christ's body, torn for us."

"Before the curtain tore, couldn't people pray to God?" Priscilla questioned.

"Yes, through a High Priest, but because God gave His promise to Abraham to be the heir of the world, (Romans 4: 13) it seemed back then that Gentiles were pretty much left out." Missfit explained.

Merkie piped in with, "That's me alright, because I'm very gentle!"

"You are that Merkie," Missfit agreed with a smile, "And I love you for it, but just so the little ones understand, a Gentile is anyone who's not a descendant of Abraham, Isaac, and Jacob.

The Bible also says the tombs broke open and the bodies of many holy people who had died were raised to life. They came out of the tombs, and after Jesus' resurrection they went into the holy city and appeared to very many people.

When the centurion and those with him who were guarding Jesus saw the earthquake and all that

had happened, they were terrified, and exclaimed, "Surely he was the Son of God!"
As evening approached, there came a rich man from Arimathea, named Joseph, who had himself become a disciple of Jesus. Going to Pilate, he asked for Jesus' body and Pilate ordered that it be given to him. Joseph took the body, wrapped it in a clean linen cloth, and placed it in his own new tomb that he had cut out of the rock. He rolled a big stone in front of the entrance to the tomb and went away."

Missfit interrupted her story, adding,
"I love the fact that the tomb stone was supernaturally rolled away because it gives us a glimpse into the invisible world that is just as real as this one.
All of us know about this physical world because it is easily seen with our eyes, but...do you all understand that there is also a spirit realm that is unseen, where God, angels, the devil, and our thoughts exist?"

Mildred, who used to be a genie, (which is a whole other story) piped up with, "Yup! I've been there!"

Nodding, Missfit continued, "Did you know also that our thoughts have tremendous power?
(Matthew 5:28) That's why God instructs us so often to guard our hearts!"

"Unless you're a bird brain like me," Vern said dejectedly. At that, Priscilla reached over and gave him a gentle love pat on his head.

92

Missfit went on, "And... prayer suggests that the human mind is also a transmission tower."

Then she challenged them, "Does anyone know which book of the Bible God's very first promise concerning His Supernatural intervention plan is found?"

"Is it Genesis?" Priscilla guessed.

"Bingo!" Missfit cheered, "Hundreds of years before Christ, in Genesis 3:15 God was actually talking to the serpent when He said, "I will put enmity between you (Satan) and the woman, (meaning Israel) and between your offspring and hers (meaning Jesus); He will crush your head, and you will strike his heel.""

Before thinking about it, Pinky blurted out, "Harley talked to a serpent this morning!"
All eyes moved to Harley, who was busy blowing out the fire at the end of his marshmallow fork. "Who likes them burnt?"
He cringed, offering a black marshmallow.

Clyde wasted no time in answering, "If you're referring to serpents, yeah, I like them' burnt! But if you're talking about that blob on your fork... no thanks!"

Deciding to devour the blackened mess himself, Harley did so, talking as he chewed, "Oh, this was a nice serpent. In fact, he said he was an under cover agent for the King Himself, King Jesus! But he disappeared so fast, I never caught his name."

"Don't you know you can't trust a talking snake Harley?" Clyde scolded, "Just look at what happened in the Garden of Eden!"

Missfit confided, "In all honesty Clyde, the serpent wasn't the only one to blow it back there in the garden. God created mankind in His image, remember? And then Genesis 1:26 says He gave Adam and Eve authority and dominion over all the earth. They handed that authority over to Satan when they agreed with his deceitful suggestion to mistrust God.
(Genesis 3:5)

Adam actually "gave away" God's ability to legally bless them and gave permission to the devil take control of their thoughts. Apparently, up until then the devil had been prohibited from transmitting into their thoughts. But it wasn't long before he found a crafty serpent that enabled him to speak forth his destructive lies. Once the serpent got Adam and Eve to agree to mistrust God, their unbelief in God's goodness swung the door wide open for Satan to beam condemnation into their thoughts.
Prior to that day, they only ever knew good thoughts, which reaped a good harvest, but from that day forward, they possessed knowledge of both good and evil….the very name God gave the forbidden tree. God knew the entrance of condemnation would bring about death and destruction because it's a spiritual law that unbelief in God's goodness ties His hands." (Matthew 13:58)

Just then, a shrill "Hoot who," startled the campfire

94

group. Looking up they saw Owl sitting in the Tulip tree. "Hoot-who, it's true... so get a clue...what ever this razor sharp mind believes...the owl will eventually do!" Owl proclaimed.

"You are a very wise owl," Missfit commented.

Merkie stopped stirring the fire. Leaning on the metal poker, he said, "It surely was LOVE that left the spirit realm and put on Flesh in order to legally enter the human race, to deliver everyone, including us Gentiles, from total slavery to the devils lies." (John 8:44)

No one saw her, but Wildthing had slipped out of the truck and now spoke up, saying, "Because of God's spiritual laws, without God's loving intervention, Satan's evil thought signals, bombarding people with constant accusations would eventually have caused everyone to self destruct."

Missfit beamed, "You're a pretty wise bird yourself Wildthing! Now...who's ready for some Bible Trivia?"

At that, Grandpa perked up, "Hit me!"

"As soon as Adam and Eve's eyes were opened to receive both good AND evil thought transmissions, what did they do?"

"That's easy," Grandpa declared, "Something told them they ought to be ashamed of themselves for being naked, so even though they were husband and wife, they sewed leaves together to cover themselves."

You know it Gramps," Missfit went on, "And the devil didn't even have to use a serpent that time. God knew that their condemnation and shame had come from somewhere other than their own thoughts too, which is why He asked them, "Who told you that you were naked?"

"Ha!" Merkie laughed, "You could say the devil is the original travel agent for guilt trips!"

"For sure," Missfit continued. "Did you know the New Testament says we are still at war against spiritual forces of evil today?
Ephesians 6:12 says, "For we are not wrestling with flesh and blood or contending only with physical opponents, but against the despotisms, against the powers, against the master spirits who are the world rulers of this present darkness, against the spirit forces of wickedness in the heavenly supernatural sphere." (Amplified)

"What's a desp-a-dism?" Tina misspoke.

"This despotism is an invisible guiding influence with the nature of a tyrant." Missfit defined.

"In other words, an evil thought that wants to rule," Grandpa wisely instructed, "That's why Jesus warned in Matthew 24:24 that deceit would be running rampant before His return."

Harley had been pondering everything the snake had told him earlier and finally broke in with, "Hey! That's exactly what that snake told me this morning!

He said the devil has already been disarmed and defeated....by Jesus, but day and night Satan still condemns and accuses misinformed people!"

"He's right on," Missfit agreed, "Satan and his demons can't do anything without using an earth suit, and I'm sad to say, there are many people who willingly let him use them today, without realizing it."

"I don't get what that's got to do with Easter!" Giggles wondered out loud.

"Everything," Missfit explained. "The Bible says Jesus came to destroy the devils work.
His shed blood stopped the curse Adam caused, and if we'll believe Him, we can resist the devil and forbid the destroyer from entering our thoughts."
(Luke 10:18-19)

"Wow!" Tina marveled, "Tell us more!"

So Missfit continued... "Matthew Chapter 28 says "After the Sabbath, at dawn on the first day of the week, Mary Magdalene and the other Mary went to look at the tomb.
There was a violent earthquake, for an angel of the Lord came down from heaven and, going to the tomb, rolled back the stone and sat on it. His appearance was like lightning, and his clothes were white as snow.
The guards were so afraid of him that they shook and became like dead men. The angel said to the women, "Do not be afraid, for I know that you are looking for Jesus, who was crucified. He is not here;

97

he has risen, just as he said. Come and see the place where he lay. Then go quickly and tell his disciples: 'He has risen from the dead and is going ahead of you into Galilee. There you will see him.' Now I have told you."

So the women hurried away from the tomb, afraid yet filled with joy, and ran to tell his disciples. Suddenly Jesus met them. "Greetings," he said. They came to him, clasped his feet and worshiped him. Then Jesus said to them, "Do not be afraid. Go and tell my brothers to go to Galilee; there they will see me."

While the women were on their way, some of the guards went into the city and reported to the chief priests everything that had happened. When the chief priests had met with the elders and devised a plan, they gave the soldiers a large sum of money, telling them, "You are to say, and 'His disciples came during the night and stole him away while we were asleep.' If this report gets to the governor, we will satisfy him and keep you out of trouble." So the soldiers took the money and did as they were instructed. And this story has been widely circulated among the Jews to this very day.

Then the eleven disciples went to Galilee, to the mountain where Jesus had told them to go. When they saw him, they worshiped him; but some doubted. Then Jesus came to them and said, "All authority in heaven and on earth has been given to me. Therefore go and make disciples of all nations, baptizing them in the name of the Father and of the Son and of the Holy Spirit, and teaching them to obey everything I have commanded you. And surely I am with you always, to the very end of the age."

Granny lifted her head off of Grandpa's shoulder and sighed, "I love that story!"

"It's true too!" Merkie boldly proclaimed. (Galatians 3:13-14)

Missfit reflected, "Once I came to realize how very much God loves me, no one could ever convince me again that He isn't completely good and totally on my side. (Luke 4:19)

"When we believe in Jesus, God declares us righteous and sends the person of the Holy Spirit to live in us. He teaches us to think like He does, and that kind of right thinking can only manifest good in our lives." (John 14: 15-17)

"Hoot who...because where ever your thoughts go, you'll follow!" Owl repeated loudly.

"Speaking of thinking," Merkie teased, "I'm thinking... it's past my bedtime!"

"Come on little ones," Grandpa stood up, "Say goodnight."

Everyone picked up their chairs saying, "See you in the morning!"

Merkie and Missfit carried the long forks and trash back up to the house, thanking God for a wonderful day with so many blessings.

God took note of their gratitude and dispatched His angels to guard their precious Possum Ranch from harm as they slept, just as He promises in His Word. (Psalm 91:9-10)

Chapter 12

Negative Ned!

The next morning, Miss Pearly Mae Possum had already gone inside to sleep for the day but Perkins was still hanging up side down by his tail in a tree when he heard a shrill, "Cock-a-doodle-doo!"

Hound Dog lumbered out of his house to bark back a greeting of his own to Ned, the very negative ranch rooster.
"Woof," He barked. Surprised to see Ned sitting on the roof of his dog house he jolted, "Or should I have said ROOF?" Getting no reaction he continued, "Hey Ned! What's up?"

"Humph, it's Monday," Ned complained, "And that makes me blue... how about you?"

"I'm very good thanks!" Hound Dog replied.

At that Ned recoiled, "Don't worry, you'll get over it."

"Gees, why are you always so negative Ned?" Hound Dog scolded, "I didn't get up and come out here to be depressed and harassed you know!"

"Oh yeah," Ned smirked, "Where do you usually go to be depressed and harassed?"

Perkins had been listening from the nearby tree and decided to have a little fun with the grouchy rooster. Racing down the trunk, he ran to Hound Dog's kennel.

"You certainly do have a great crowing talent," He said, looking up at the rude rooster still perched on the roof of Hound Dog's house.

"Why thank you," Ned said, sticking out his chest.

Reaching out his paw and holding something up Perkins asked, "Want to buy some lip gloss? It's my own invention."

Ned sneered, "What kind of lip gloss?"
"Moose manure lip gloss," Perkins grinned.

Enunciating slowly with disgust, Ned said, "Moose Manure lip gloss, that couldn't possibly work!"

"Well," Said Perkins, through a huge smile, "I don't know whether or not it works, but it shore keeps you from licking' your lips!"

Deciding to join in the fun, Hound Dog asked Ned, "Does a Rooster have lips?"

Strutting to the far side of the roof Ned griped, "You must think I'm a perfect idiot!"

Without any hesitation at all Perkins came back with, "Nope...no one's perfect!"

"Cock-a-doodle-doo," Ned screeched again, this time adding, "I'm sick and tired of you!"

Inside the house, squinting to read his clock Merkie thought, "Five a.m. and Ned's mad already?"

Just then another piercing "Cock-a-doodle-doo, I've had it with all of you," was heard by all, signaling that morning had definitely arrived and that this day, Ned was even more negative than usual, if that were possible.

"I think Ned got up on the wrong side of the bed," Missfit surmised, raising her head up off of her pillow.

"Maybe he needs to be fed!" Merkie joked with a twinkle in his eye.

Catching on, Missfit continued, "Or perhaps he's been dropped on his head!"

"Cock-a-doodle-doo...Wake up, all of you!"

"I'd better go speak to him," Merkie offered as he finished helping Missfit make the bed.

"I'll put the coffee on," She said, hearing, "Cock-a-doodle-do, now get up! All of you!"

"That's strange, it sounds like he's in the dog kennel," Merkie contemplated.

Grabbing some dog biscuits he went towards Hound Dog's kennel. Seeing Ned on the roof of the dog house he asked, "What's up Nedly?"

"Everyone better be!" Ned bragged as he strutted.

"You did good," Merkie complimented, "In fact, I think you may have woke the dead over in the cemetery."

"Thanks, I love you too," Ned half ways smiled.

Always ready with a punch line, Perkins looked at Ned and risked, "And we love you too Ned, in fact, I love you even more today than I did yesterday. Yesterday you really kind of got on my nerves."

"Maybe if you'd sleep at night like the rest of us you wouldn't have trouble with your nerves!" Ned snapped.

"Nedly," Merkie said, "I'm detecting that you are upset about something today."

"I'm just sick and tired of it!" Ned cut loose, "I know everyone calls me ole negative Ned, but you'd be negative too if you had to be the first one to get up at the crack of dawn, day in and day out. I'm sick and tired of being alone too. Maybe if I had a hen and a family I wouldn't be so negative."

At that, Hound Dog piped up, "MAYBE if you weren't so negative you'd attract rather than repel a hen, as well as everyone else!"

Leaning on the fence post and sticking a tooth pick in his mouth Merkie pondered, "You know what guys....I know of a particular little girl who had many good reasons to be sad and negative, but today she's the happiest person I know."

Ned was listening intently, "Go on."

Merkie continued, "Because of a bitter divorce she was never allowed to know her dad or any of his family. Her mom raised her alone and had to work every day. This caused the little girl to have to spend many days feeling like an outsider while being cared for in other people's homes.

She was not only poor, but because of a false belief system her mother lived in constant fear. Consequently she was very strict and wouldn't allow the little girl to associate with other children or join them in doing normal childhood activities. This gave the little girl such a distorted view of life and God; she spent every day wishing she'd never been born.

You see, she perceived God to be just like her dad. She saw both of them as being responsible for giving her life, but it seemed to her that neither one of them was willing to lift a finger to help her live it.

This wrong belief caused her to resent God and everyone else.

When she grew up and got married and had kids of her own, she finally did get to meet her father, but then just six days later her mother died. Then because her husband was unfaithful she found herself divorced and completely alone. Thinking no one, not even God cared, she spent the next several years running as far away from God as she could."

"Whoa!" Ned exclaimed, "That IS sad!"

"It gets worse too," Merkie went on, "She went from one bad relationship to another looking for someone who'd love her, only to nearly lose her life one night at the hands of the man she loved.

But then something wonderful happened right in the middle of what she thought would be her last breath! The same God she'd resented her entire life came to her at that moment. He actually spoke into her heart, saying that she'd believed a lie and needed to find out the truth.

The very next day she got help from a friend who took time to sit down with her and show her from a real undistorted Bible what the real truth about the nature of God is. Here's what she learned."

Galatians 3:22
"The Scriptures picture all mankind as shut up and imprisoned by sin, so that the inheritance and blessing which was promised through faith in Jesus Christ the Messiah might be released, delivered, and committed to all those who believe, adhere to, trust in and rely on Him."

John 3:16
"For God so greatly loved and dearly prized the

world that He even gave up His only begotten unique Son, so that whoever believes in, trusts in, clings to and relies on Him shall not perish or come to destruction and be lost but have eternal everlasting life."

"And...?" Ned asked.

"And..." Merkie straightened up, "She went to God that very night and told Him that she wasn't running away from Him any more.

She realized it had been an enemy that had caused her to believe lies about God. That truth set her free, and today God is her Abba Father." (Romans 8:15 and Galatians 4:5-6)

"And He's the best Father a girl could ever hope for!"

All four friends whirled around to see that Missfit had walked up behind them.

Throwing down his toothpick and holding out his arms towards her, Merkie added, "And here's that girl right now."

Ned and Perkins and Hound Dog looked on at the clown couple standing there in each others arms, when Perkins broke the silence.
"Land sakes, were you talking about Missfit?"

"None other," Merkie beamed.

"You shore are happy today," Perkins perceived.

Looking rather serious, especially for a blue haired clown, Merkie started, "It hasn't always been so. From the beginning we thought our love for each other would carry us through anything, but after awhile life threw us some curves that made just getting through a day difficult sometimes. We both got into trouble because we'd began focusing on all of the things we could see rather than on our great God."

Missfit offered, "If more people only knew exactly what all Jesus meant when He said "It is finished," they'd go running to Him.
It's why we do what we do today. I was so lost and miserable when I couldn't believe God loved me. I saw myself as a misfit...and where the mind goes, the girl follows!

"Yup," Merkie declared as he gave Missfit a squeeze, "We're living proof that Jesus turns beauty into ashes!"

Ned blurted out, "Well, one of you is anyway," But added quickly, "Just kidding."

Everyone laughed out loud, including Ned, "Oh alright, I'll change my tune. How's this," Clearing his throat, "Cock-A-Doodle-Do...It's time to start anew!"

Giving Missfit a wink, Merkie turned to Perkins, "Speaking of starting anew, how about we begin working on your house today?"

"WOW," Perkins said, "I've been up all night but I'll give it a shot! Suppose yawl could help me out Ned?"

"Cock-A-Doodle-Do" Ned agreed, "I'll crow all day for you."

Not to be outdone, Hound Dog responded with, "Woof woof woof, you can do it from my roof."

Shrugging his shoulders, Merkie said to Ned, "It doesn't rhyme, but I'll let you know if any hens move into the neighborhood."

"Good enough!" Ned gladly consented.

"Coffee on the patio in 5 minutes," Missfit informed as she headed for the house, thanking God silently in her heart for the blessing of Jesus, Merkie, and even Ned in her life.

God took note of her gratitude and planned an awesome surprise for her later that very day.

Made in the USA